You must believe me when I tell you that I have found it impossible to carry the heavy burden of responsibility and to discharge my duties as King as I would wish to do without the help and support of the woman I love.'

Behind the words that Edward VIII spoke to the nation on that historic day in 1936, lay a love affair that not only condemned the King and his bride to a life of exile but also shook the very foundations of the British monarchy.

WORLDS APART

DAVID AND WALLIS GREW UP ON OPPOSITE SIDES OF THE WORLD. BUT THEY WERE ALREADY SET ON A COLLISION COURSE THAT WAS TO SHAKE HISTORY

Hulton-Deutsch Collection

THE DUKE AND DUCHESS OF WINDSOR MADE the most unlikely and extraordinary couple, for before fortune and destiny combined to bring them together, they could not have led more different lives. While the Duke was born into the pomp and splendour of the British Royal Family, the Duchess – two years his junior – had a turbulent childhood in America.

The Empire was at its illustrious peak at the time of the future King Edward VIII's birth on 23 June 1894 and large crowds cheered Queen Victoria all the way as she travelled to White Lodge in Richmond Park to visit her great-grandson and his parents, the Duke and Duchess of York. The baby was called Edward Albert Christian George Andrew Patrick David, but would always be known within the family circle as David.

'Wretched childhood'

Soon after the birth, the family and its entourage of servants moved to York Cottage on the Royal Estate of Sandringham in Norfolk, and it was here that the young David was to spend much of his 'wretched childhood', as he referred to it in later years.

Over the next few years, the Duchess gave birth to five more children – Prince Albert, who became King George VI, Princess Mary, and the Princes Henry, George, and lastly John, who was to die tragically young from epilepsy.

When the Duke and Duchess paid an official visit to Australia in 1901, the children were sent to stay with their grandparents at the 'big house' on the Sandringham estate. The Prince (later King Edward VII) and Princess of Wales doted on their grandchildren, but even during those happy times, David, or Edward as he was more formally called, was prone to be melancholic. Lord Esher, a friend of the family, noted that 'Edward is a most charming boy ... but the look of world-weariness in his eyes, I cannot

trace to any ancestor of the House of Hanover.'

When David was eight and Albert ('Bertie') six, their grandfather was crowned King, becoming Edward VII, and their parents became the Prince and Princess of Wales. The two elder boys were entrusted to the care of Frederick Finch, a footman and trusted friend. Then another less happy influence entered their lives: their tutor, Henry Hansell, who seems to have been peculiarly ill-suited to his job.

The Navy and Oxford

In 1907, just before his 13th birthday, David entered the Royal Naval College at Osborne House on the Isle of Wight (formerly Queen Victoria's residence). The shocks of Osborne

Hulton-Deutsch Collection

♛ *A future king was born on 23 June 1894. Although Edward was his formal name, he was always David to family and close friends. Two years after his birth, on 19 June 1896, Wallis below right was born in Pennsylvania. Shortly afterwards, her father died and Wallis and her mother returned south to Baltimore. As Duchess of Windsor, Wallis later wrote: 'In spite of the accident of my Pennsylvania birth, I always considered myself a Southerner'*

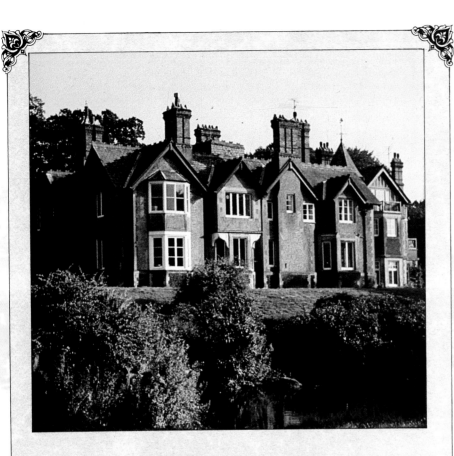

YORK COTTAGE

No bigger than a small vicarage, York Cottage on the Sandringham estate in Norfolk was a warren of tiny, over-furnished rooms. Sounds echoed all around the house and young David felt lonely, cold and unloved there

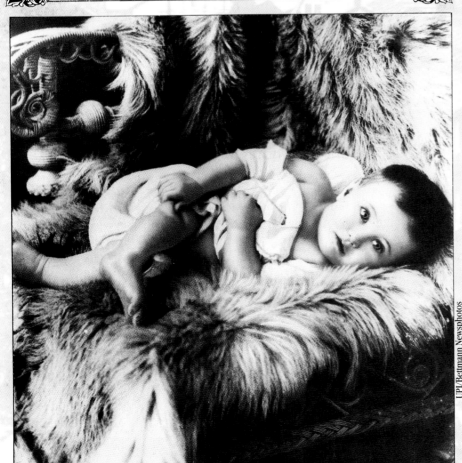

UPI/Bettmann Newsphotos

came hard and fast to the sheltered Prince. Academically, he started to fall behind. Engineering, navigation and science were new subjects to him and he was ill-equipped to tackle them. Hansell had taught him and his brother virtually nothing of any value.

After two years, he graduated to the senior Royal Naval College at Dartmouth which was more to his liking. But in May 1910, his grandfather died and his father became King. The new King, George V, decided to make his son the Prince of Wales and David was forced to leave Dartmouth before graduating. He had just started to enjoy Navy life, and it was a bitter blow.

The Coronation of the new King took place on 22 June 1911 and the young Prince, dressed in full regalia, was one of the first to pay homage to his father. 'I, Edward Prince of Wales, do become your liege man of life and limb and of earthly worship,' he pledged.

The 'Baltimore heartbreaker'

At about this time, a hitherto rather reserved and modest American girl was beginning to blossom into a charismatic young woman. As a debutante in her late teens, Wallis Warfield earned the nickname of the 'Baltimore heartbreaker'. But she had not always been so confident and cheerful.

Wallis was born in Pennsylvania on 19 June 1896, a year after her mother, Alice Montague, had married the curiously named Teackle Warfield. She was baptized Bessiewallis Warfield, following the Baltimore custom of amalgamating two names to form one. In her teenage years, she dropped the Bessie because she said it 'reminded her of cows'.

Teackle had taken his pregnant wife to a health resort in Pennsylvania in search of a cure for his tuberculosis; to no avail, for he died just five months after the baby was born. This tragedy put Alice and her infant daughter in the position of poor and dependent relations.

In later years, the Duchess of Windsor would be incensed at suggestions that she was 'from the wrong side of the tracks'. Her ancestors on both sides of the family had been distinguished English settlers, and one genealogist has traced her lineage as far back as King Edward III of England.

Although the Montagues had the breeding that was considered all-important in the Southern states, they did not have the money to support the name. The Warfield family, on the other hand, had made 'new' money in banking and insurance, and cared little for the niceties of social class. It was not surprising, then, that when Alice married the sickly Teackle she was suspected of chasing the Warfield fortune.

After Teackle's death, mother and child were taken in by granny Warfield, his widowed

UPI/Bettmann Newsphotos

👑 Above *Wallis, aged six months, with Alice Warfield. Wallis later credited her mother with 'a flashing wit and a bubbling gaiety'*

👑 *The Princes and Princess in 1901. From left to right Mary, Albert (later George VI), David, Henry and seated baby George*

mother. Her vast house in Preston Street in the middle of Baltimore was kept by 'Uncle Sol', Teackle's millionaire brother Solomon.

Alice and Bessiewallis were later taken in by Alice's elder sister, Bessie Montague Merryman. Then Alice rented an apartment and took in 'dinner guests'. After a few years, the family moved again, to a rented house where Alice took in boarders. This was not so readily accepted by polite society who viewed it as too lowly an occupation for a woman with such an historic name. But Alice's income helped to balance her books and she managed to send Bessiewallis to Arundell, a private school.

Bessiewallis was well liked by her schoolmates at Arundell. She was naturally witty, if rather reserved. Even during these early years, however, she was considered 'fast'.

In 1908, Alice Warfield was married for the second time, to John Freeman Raisin, the son of a wealthy Baltimore politician. For the first time the family enjoyed a degree of affluence, and Wallis could at last afford the sort of clothes that set off her growing sophistication.

Hulton-Deutsch Collection

TESTAMENT OF YOUTH

Coronation fever gripped Britain throughout the summer of 1911. After the crowning of George V in Westminster Abbey, the King and Queen and the Royal children toured the country, to the delight of the people. The climax of this Royal cavalcade was to be the Investiture of the Heir Apparent at Caernarvon Castle in Wales.

The significance of the occasion was not lost on 16-year-old David, but he was also beset by doubts and fears. By his own account, 'when a tailor appeared to measure me up for a fantastic costume of white satin breeches and a mantle and surcoat of purple velvet edged with ermine, I decided things had gone too far … what would my Navy friends say if they saw me in this preposterous rig?'

A crowd of 11,000 crammed themselves inside the castle walls to hear Winston Churchill proclaim the Prince's titles. They waited in hushed silence until the King presented him on the battlements, then they cheered him spontaneously. 'The dear boy did it all remarkably well and looked so nice,' the King wrote.

David loathed being a 'person requiring homage' and was 'desperately anxious to be treated exactly like any other boy of my age'.

'Bookish he will never be'

David had a spell at sea, as a midshipman aboard the battleship HMS *Hindustan,* an interlude that lasted only three months and failed to mature him as his father had hoped. Undeterred, King George came up with another plan. He decided that David should study at Oxford University. The idea of Oxford alarmed David; he knew he was not a learned man but all his protests fell on deaf ears. The entrance exam was waived, Lord Derby's son was chosen as companion for the Prince, and Magdalen was chosen as the college.

At the beginning, David was lonely there but he rapidly became popular and well respected. He wore extravagant jackets with loud checks and fashionable trousers. And, instead of exploiting his status, he accepted friendship on merit, steadfastly defying his father's wish that he should circulate only with Old Etonians. He knew a future king had no need of a degree and the charming and handsome Prince left Oxford with a remark from the President of Magdalen College that he treasured for the rest of his life: 'Bookish he will never be.'

👑 *Wallis Warfield* above left *with Mary Kirk, who became Ernest Simpson's third wife. They were classmates at Oldfields* right

👑 *The new Prince of Wales suffered through his Investiture at Caernarvon* below – *'a sufficient ordeal for anyone,' he called it*

The Daily Mirror

nearly lost his life. But David remained determined to visit the troops and won the overwhelming admiration of the ordinary soldier – the saying went round: 'A bad shelling will always produce the Prince of Wales.' Even the King acknowledged his son's bravery and insisted he wear the medals he had been given. David refused as he found it distasteful to wear medals awarded in peacetime.

Whilst on leave in 1915, the Prince fell in love for the first time. He was 21 and the object of his affections, Lady Coke, was 12 years his senior. She was also married. The affair lasted for three years; they saw each other frequently when he was on leave and, while he was away, he poured out his love to her in hundreds of letters.

David's Royal tours

In the spring of 1916, the Prince of Wales was sent to the Middle East to inspect the defences of Suez. Here, he met the Australian and New Zealand troops who had been evacuated from the disaster at Gallipoli. Later the next year, he went on a morale-boosting trip to Italy, and towards the end of the war travelled through France, Germany and Belgium to visit the troops.

On his return to England at the end of the war, he met Freda Dudley Ward, who was to become his next great passion.

At the age of 16, just as war was brewing in Europe, Wallis Warfield had gone to Oldfields, a finishing school on the outskirts of Baltimore. She was rapidly maturing into a desirable young woman, and she had very definite social ambitions. But in 1910 her stepfather, John Raisin, had died, leaving a pitifully small inheritance, and Alice had had little option but to return to the boarding house business. In the meantime Uncle Sol paid for Wallis's schooling.

A father substitute

Sol was certainly not a man to be parted from his money easily, but he was a constant factor in Wallis's life in the absence of a real father. Consequently, it came of something of a shock to Wallis when the *Baltimore Sun* carried the following announcement: 'The report that I will give a large ball for my debutante niece, Miss Wallis Warfield, is without foundation in that I do not consider the present a proper time for such festivities, when thousands of men are being slaughtered in Europe.'

The year was 1914 and Wallis was by now a vivacious young lady who bragged at school and in the many homes she visited that she was

During the spring of 1914, the rumblings of impending war grew steadily louder. In June, David came down from Oxford and went straight into the 1st Life Guards. The reason for his swift posting was 'to improve his seat on a horse'. Once more, the King was wielding his influence on his son. He was afraid that people might see David as a 'duffer' when he went out fox-hunting. The Guards was hard work for the Prince but his confidence grew.

When war broke out, David was not allowed to accompany his regiment to France. But his persistence won through and, when he got his first taste of life in the trenches, he and it was now that she earned the tag of being a heartbreaker. She had no pretentions to being pretty, but did know how to dress and she was, above everything else, charming.

When she was almost 20, Wallis took herself off to Florida for a spring break. She went to see a Montague cousin, Corinne Mustin, who was married to a naval officer. She talked with Corinne of her many beaux, the men who had pursued her over the past few years. Unimpressed, Corinne asked her husband to bring home his friends to meet her cousin.

First acceptance

Lieutenant Earl Winfield Spencer captured Wallis's heart at their first meeting. The dashing pilot in the air arm of the US Navy 'swallowed her up,' and the attraction was mutual.

Wallis lingered at the house near Pensacola for months, paying her way with good humour and wit rather than money. Win, as she was to call her new hero, eventually proposed on the veranda of the Pensacola Country Club. She hesitated before accepting. It was a decision that had profound consequences.

going to enjoy her very own 'coming-out' ball. She was immensely disappointed. But there were plenty of other balls to attend.

Coming-out balls in 1914 had one sole purpose for the affluent girls of Baltimore – to find an eligible man. Her suitors thought Wallis 'charming' and 'fast' – words of high praise –

👑 *David's undergraduate days at Oxford were happier than he had expected. On his own admission he was not a great scholar, but he enjoyed playing sport and was an active member of the University Officer Training Corps* top. *He is shown* above *leaving Magdalen College with his tutor, Henry Hansell, in the autumn of 1912*

👑 *Debutante Wallis Warfield 'came out' at the Bachelor's Cotillion Ball in 1914. From the moment the invitation dropped through her letterbox, she said, 'I was lost to all other earthly considerations'*

THE GREAT WAR

The Prince of Wales was infuriated at the decision to prevent him joining his Life Guards regiment on the Western Front. 'What does it matter if I am killed?' he asked War Secretary Lord Kitchener. 'I have four brothers.' Kitchener replied that he could not risk the Heir Apparent being taken prisoner. But, in due course, the Prince got his way. He spent much of the next four years making morale-boosting visits to Allied troops across Europe, gaining 'some idea of the horror and ghastliness of it all'. His willingness to brave the war zones and his encouragement of factory workers on the Home Front earned him the gratitude of the nation

Hulton-Deutsch Collection

Hulton-Deutsch Collection

Popperfoto

From Warfield to Windsor

Richard Warfield
of Berkshire
(circa 1650)

Peter Montague
of Bovency,
Buckinghamshire
(b. 1603)

Albert of Saxe-Coburg m. Queen Victoria
and Gotha   (1819-1901)
(1819-1861)

Henry Mactier m. Anna Emory
Warfield   (d. 1915)
(1825-1885)

Alexandra,   m. King Edward VII
Princess of Denmark   (1841-1910)
(1844-1925)

Daniel
Warfield   Teackle Wallis m. Alice Montague
Richard Emory   Warfield   (d. 1929)
Warfield   (1869-1896)

Princess Mary of m. King George V
Teck   (1865-1936)
(1867-1953)

Solomon Davies
Warfield
(1859-1927)

Wallis Warfield
Simpson
(1896-1986)

David,
King Edward VIII
(1894-1972)
(abd. 1936)

King George VI
(1895-1952)

Mary,
Princess Royal

Henry,
Duke of Gloucester

George,
Duke of Kent

Prince John

👑 **All dressed up – David aged two**

👑 **With sister Mary, the future Princess Royal, in 1901**

👑 **As a chorus 'girl' in the operetta HMS Pinafore,** *1901*

👑 **In the bos'n's chair – sailing off Cowes aged 12**

👑 **Bicycling at Balmoral in 1911**

Mary McPherson, Baltimore

☗ *Cutting a dash – Wallis in her early teens*

UPI/Bettmann Newsphotos

☗ *Looking pensive – Wallis aged two*

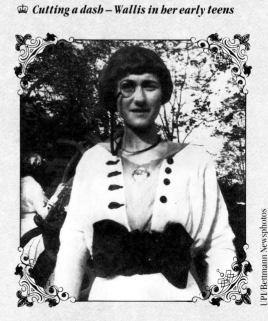

UPI/Bettmann Newsphotos

☗ *A monocled Miss Wallis Warfield*

UPI/Bettmann Newsphotos

☗ *Wallis right, with cousin – Baltimore, 1899*

☗ *Enjoying a sleigh ride at Lake Placid in 1898*

UPI/Bettmann Newsphotos

God Bless The Prince of Wales

The title 'Prince of Wales' is an ancient one, going back more than 600 years, but investitures at Caernarvon Castle are comparatively infrequent. Edward's took place in 1911, when he had reached the age of 16, and was the first such ceremony at Caernarvon since 1616. When King George V placed the circlet on his son's head, he could scarcely have imagined that this was the only crown Edward was destined to wear

ILN Picture Library

♛ The Prince's circlet *above* was made of Welsh gold, set with freshwater pearls and amethysts

♛ For the Investiture, Edward wore a velvet doublet and mantle over white satin knee breeches – and the Order of the Garter

♛ The head of the rod of office *below* has three cherubs holding an amethyst-centred coronet

♛ Two fantastic dragons, holding a coronet, form the hilt of the ceremonial sword. The scabbard is covered in purple velvet

His Royal Highness Edward Albert Christian George Andrew Patrick David Prince of Wales Duke of Cornwall and Rothsay Earl of Chester and Carrick Baron of Renfrew Lord of the Isles and Great Steward of Scotland.

♛ Rich with symbolism, the Royal Arms include the Imperial Crown and the Order of the Garter with the Royal Supporters, the lion and the unicorn standing on either side. The Prince of Wales feathers *top left*, three ostrich plumes surmounting the motto *Ich dien* (I serve), are supposed by legend to have been taken from the dead King of Bohemia at the battle of Crécy in 1346

♛ The ring features two dragons clasping an amethyst – Edward's name can be glimpsed inside

ILN Picture Library

ENGLAND EXPECTS

DURING THE ROARING TWENTIES, THE PRINCE OF WALES AND WALLIS SIMPSON WERE BOTH UNLUCKY IN LOVE. WHEN THEY FINALLY MET, THEY WERE RASH ENOUGH TO BELIEVE THEY WOULD FIND PEACE TOGETHER

ILN Picture Library

IT WAS TO BE 12 YEARS BEFORE DAVID MET his future wife. In that time, both travelled the globe and both fell in and out of love. Their meeting, when it came, quickly led to a deep mutual passion.

By the end of the Great War the 25-year-old Prince of Wales was still deeply in love with Freda Dudley Ward, whom he had met in unlikely circumstances, during an air-raid.

Lady Asquith misleadingly described Freda as a 'pretty little fluff'. In fact, she was a mature, intelligent and charming woman. The affair lasted for 16 years and, although it was always discreet, it could never be kept entirely secret.

Anxious for a measure of independence from his parents, after the war the Prince moved to York House in St James's Palace. But he was rarely there because, for the next six years until 1925, he spent much of his time travelling the world, thanking the peoples of the British Empire for their contribution to the war effort.

Wherever he went, his reputation as a war

ILN Picture Library

Topham Picture Library

One of the joys of the Indian tour was his meeting with Captain Edward 'Fruity' Metcalfe who turned out to be a loyal friend and confidant for much of his life. He even had a 'fling' with Metcalfe's wife, Alexandra.

With a reputation for having 'a girl in every port', the Prince enjoyed the popularity of a film star. But this gave him little satisfaction, for privately he was a lonely figure who found it hard to form deep personal relationships with women who were not 'safely' married to other men in his circle.

The bored batchelor

When not travelling as the King's envoy around the world, he mingled with London's Society Set. He dressed in outlandish clothes and took to wearing a top hat at a rakish angle, much to the displeasure of the King. A royal courtier is said to have heard the King bellowing furiously at his eldest son: 'You dress like a cad. You act like a cad. You are a cad. Get out!'

His mother remained regally distant. He received little sympathy from her when, 'smoking one cigarette after another and talking his heart out,' he told her he wanted to fulfil his royal role in his own way, as a 'modern man'.

During the General Strike of 1926, the Prince showed genuine concern for the plight of the working man, but his ignorance of contemporary politics was obvious.

Loved as he was by the public at large, those closest to him began to tire of his immaturity and thoughtlessness. He could not disguise the fact that he was easily bored and, if he did not want to do something, he did not do it. On one occasion, he was not above keeping the Prime Minister, Stanley Baldwin, and his wife waiting for a dinner engagement while he completed a game of squash.

In 1930, the Prince bought a mansion near

♛ *During her first husband's posting to California, vivacious naval wife Wallis Spencer was much in demand for beach parties and weekend gatherings. Her smile hid the fact that the marriage was coming under increasing strain*

hero and fun-lover preceded him. He was the first royal personage to mingle with the people and he was never afraid to entertain them. But the pressures inevitably began to take their toll. During the 1921 tour of the Indian subcontinent, Lord Louis Mountbatten, his cousin who accompanied him on the trip, commented, 'I soon realized that under that delightful smile . . . he was a lonely and sad person, always liable to deep depression.'

THE PRINCE'S AMOURS

The Prince of Wales enjoyed close relationships with some of the most beautiful women of his day, including *from left to right* Lady Rosemary Leveson-Gower, Mrs Freda Dudley Ward, Lady Diana Cooper and Lady Thelma Furness. Rosemary Leveson-Gower was the only unmarried woman in whom he ever showed more than a passing interest. Another friend, Lady Alexandra Metcalfe, remarked shrewdly, 'The Prince always liked . . . married women . . . He wasn't interested in girls of his own age'

Sunningdale, deep in the Berkshire countryside, called Fort Belvedere. He saw the 'pseudo-Gothic hodge-podge' as a retreat where he could relax with his friends.

A disillusioned bride

In 1916, Wallis married for the first time. She wore a white velvet dress and her head was crowned with a lace veil. Her groom, Winfield Spencer, and his comrades wore their dashing naval uniforms and, to complete her happiness, Uncle Sol gave her away. But the discovery, on their wedding night, that her husband was a heavy drinker came as a deep shock to Wallis.

Their first home was a cottage near Pensacola in the 'sunshine' state of Florida. But, sadly, the marriage had started on a cool note and it never fully recovered. Wallis repeatedly begged Win, as she called him, to do something about his chronic drink problem but to no avail.

For consolation she led a determinedly carefree life as a party-goer. But this only made Win passionately jealous, and drove him deeper into the abyss of alcoholism.

They did not stay long in Florida. Win was posted to Boston, then, in 1920, to San Diego (where, at a naval reception, she curtseyed to the visiting Prince of Wales), and then Washington DC. Here she found herself in her element. While she enjoyed the social life of the capital at dances and parties, Win consoled himself with drink. Win thought the nightmare would end when he received a posting to Hong Kong, but Wallis, much to the consternation of

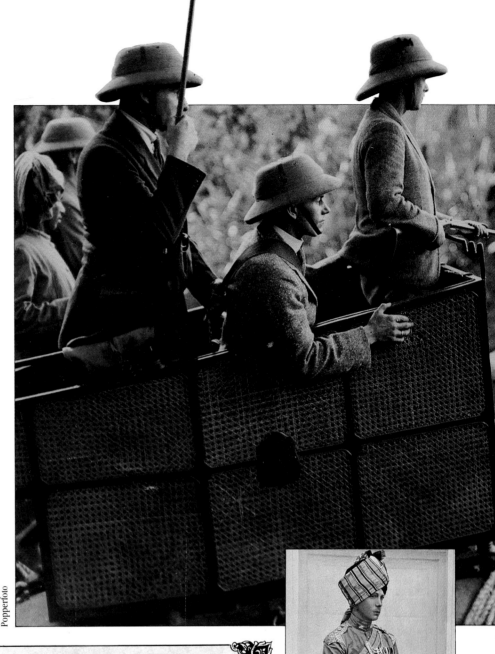

Popperfoto

MARRIED IN HASTE

'An unusually well-balanced man,' was Wallis's verdict on second husband Ernest Simpson *left*. He gave her the stable home life missing from her first marriage to Lieutenant Winfield Spencer *below*. The pioneering aviator who had swept her off her feet had proved to be an unpredictable drunkard. On one occasion, he had locked Wallis in the bathroom for several hours while he went on a drinking spree

UPI/Bettmann Newsphotos

Hulton-Deutsch Collection

Topham Picture Library

♛ *The world tours that the Prince of Wales undertook after the Great War left him exhausted. Tiger hunting in Nepal* top *was a welcome respite from official functions* above *and the cheery company of Louis Mountbatten* top right *kept his spirits up*

Popperfoto

The 'Jazz Age' – the era of flappers and 'bright young things' – was at its height when the new Mrs Simpson took up residence in London. She was soon moving in the highest circles

ILN Picture Library

her family, refused to accompany him.

After considering a divorce from Winfield Spencer, Wallis succumbed to his pleas for a reconciliation and set sail – with considerable misgivings – for China. The attempted reconciliation soon failed; when Win came home drunk from an evening at a 'sing-song' house, she left and never spent another night with her husband.

Wallis, who was approaching 30, spent the next two years on the move, hopping from city to city, living off her greatest asset, her charm. A few happy months were spent in Peking with new-found friends, the Rogers, but by 1926 she had tired of China and returned home to discover that her mother had married for the third time. The following year, her divorce from Winfield Spencer was granted in Virginia.

Just before her divorce came through, Wallis received news that her rich Uncle Sol had died. She received a modest settlement in his will. With his death came a certain amount of freedom and Wallis visited Washington and New York for social occasions. And, during one dinner party at the Raffrays in New York, she met Mr and Mrs Ernest Simpson.

The Simpsons' marriage had been going through difficult times and within months of Wallis's divorce, the Simpsons, too, were estranged. When Ernest Simpson proposed to Wallis, she went off to France to think it over. But she had soon made up her mind – she joined him in London where he worked for his family's shipping business, and they were soon married.

The newlyweds moved to Bryanston Court and Wallis was at last able to fulfil some of her social ambitions. She was befriended by American expatriates who were attached to the embassy and she was also 'taken over' by her sister-in-law, Mrs Maud Kerr-Smiley, who was well acquainted with London's Society Set.

Another well-connected friend was Viscountess Thelma Furness who, as everyone knew, was the current close friend of the Prince of Wales. On 10 January 1931, David met Wallis Simpson for the first time at Thelma Furness's country house, Burrough Court, near Melton Mowbray in Leicestershire. Wallis and Ernest were only invited at the last minute, when another guest cried off. When she arrived at the house, there was a nerve-racking wait for the Prince of Wales to appear.

First impressions

Accompanied by his brother, Prince George, David walked into the room. The Duchess of Windsor, recalling the occasion, wrote, 'I remember thinking ... how much like his pictures he really was – the slightly wind-rumpled golden hair, the turned-up nose and a strange, wistful, almost sad look about the eyes.'

A SOCIETY AFFAIR

In January 1932, Mr and Mrs Ernest Simpson received an invitation 'clean out of the blue' to spend a weekend as guests of the Prince of Wales at Fort Belvedere. Wallis was anxious at the prospect. She worried about what she should wear and what she should say. Ernest would not hear her protestations and was keen to see the Prince and how he lived his extravagant life.

On the first evening, the Prince explained to the fascinated Wallis his 'secret vice' for doing needlepoint. Wallis recalled later: 'I decided there and then that he must have a really sweet and tender side to his nature.'

Meanwhile, the Prince was bringing to an end his close attachments to Lady Furness and Freda Dudley Ward. 'Look after the Prince of Wales for me,' were Thelma Furness's parting words to Wallis when she left on a trip to America.

When she returned, the Prince's feelings towards Thelma had obviously cooled. Finally, in the words of the Duchess of Windsor, Thelma Furness 'asked me point-blank if the Prince was interested in me – "keen" was the word she used. This was a question I had expected, and I was able to give a straight answer. "Thelma," I said, "I think he likes me."'

The 'perfect woman'

During 1932, Wallis and the Prince of Wales saw little of each other. The Simpsons' fortunes fluctuated from good to bad – Ernest's business was picking up again after the Wall Street Crash, but this often took him away on long business trips and Wallis's health was not good. Her friends, however, were loyal and, early in 1933, her American confidante, Mrs Thaw, took her down to Fort Belvedere on several occasions. These visits were informal and offered Wallis and the Prince the opportunity to get to know each other better. In June, the Prince gave a party in honour of Wallis's 37th birthday at Quaglino's, a London nightspot, and by the end of the year he knew he had found his 'perfect woman'.

As the relationship developed, the Prince became a frequent visitor to Bryanston Court, and on several occasions arrived at the flat unannounced. Ernest Simpson was not stupid and, not surprisingly, his resentment grew. He began to make himself absent, claiming that his business called him away. Slowly, the Simpsons' marriage deteriorated, and Ernest started an affair with Mary Raffray at whose party in

John Hillelson Agency

New York he had first met Wallis, and who was eventually to become his third wife.

In the summer of 1934, the Prince invited both the Simpsons to join his party of friends for a cruising holiday in Biarritz. Ernest declined but Wallis eagerly accepted. By now, she knew that the Prince's affections were genuine – she had the 'catch of a generation' within her grasp. In her own words, he had 'crossed the line that marks the indefinable boundary between friendship and love'.

When she returned to England, Ernest asked politely after the trip. 'It was like being Wallis in Wonderland,' she exulted, but she did not tell him of the Prince's present of a diamond and emerald trinket. For his part, Ernest thought it was more 'an excursion into the realm of Peter Pan's Never-Never land'.

The following spring, Wallis was again a guest of the Prince, on a skiing holiday at Kitzbuhel in Austria. Throwing caution to the wind, the Prince extended the holiday to take in Vienna and Budapest. The King was infuriated by his son's arrogance, as several official engagements had to be cancelled. It appeared

> *'He crossed the line that marks the boundary between friendship and love'*
>
> WALLIS SIMPSON

as if the Prince was openly divorcing himself from his obligations.

On their return to England, Wallis had to face up to the fact that a confrontation with Ernest was inevitable. She wrote in a letter to the Prince, 'I know that you aren't really selfish or thoughtless at heart but your life has been such that you have been the one considered, so that quite naturally you only think of what you want and take it too without the slightest thought of others ... God bless WE and be kind to me in the years to come for I have lost something noble for a boy who may always remain Peter Pan.'

By now, the Prince and Wallis had established their own 'language'. In letters they wrote of WE, meaning Wallis and Edward, and 'make oooh!', meaning to hug and cuddle in an affectionate, not sexual, kind of way.

1935 was the year of King George V's Silver Jubilee and the celebrations up and down the country were lavish and joyous. But then the King fell ill. The bronchial trouble that had plagued him for many years was winning the battle. He died at Sandringham on 20 January 1936. On the instant of his death, the Prince of Wales became King Edward VIII.

♛ *By 1935, the Prince of Wales and his new love were becoming* **inseparable** *left.* **They spent all of Ascot week together** *above,* **and she was a regular visitor to his Fort Belvedere retreat**

♛ *The new King Edward VIII, flanked by his brothers, follows his father's coffin from the church at Sandringham in January 1936*

'Straw hat trimmed with pink and blue coq feathers'

Blue crêpe gloves opening on ring finger

THE WINDSOR STYLE

Never a classic beauty, the Duchess of Windsor had a face that was charitably described as 'amusing', but her pencil-slim figure and broad shoulders allowed clothes to flatter her. A superb sense of style kept her on the list of 'best dressed' women for decades. She preferred simple designs as backgrounds for her fabulous jewels. The Duke, too, was a fashion innovator – he favoured unstructured clothes and daring combinations of colour

♔ For her quiet wedding at the Château de Candé, Wallis wore a slender dress in sapphire blue crêpe, with matching long-sleeved jacket, by the famous American designer, Mainbocher

♔ Art Déco-style brooch in sapphires and diamonds, by Van Cleef and Arpels, which Wallis pinned at the throat of her wedding ensemble

Gently flared skirt from knee to hem

♔ The Duke was married in morning dress – Wallis wears his love tokens on each wrist

Popperfoto

Ruby and diamond necklace

Lobster-pink midriff band, shaped into the waist

👑 This flawless emerald ring was bought from Cartier in 1936, on the day that Wallis's divorce proceedings began. She wears it with both the striking outfits *above*

The perfectly balanced 'Windsor-Knot' invented by the Duke himself always remained immaculate

White chiffon with hand-painted lobster motif

👑 Wallis appreciated the wit of Paris designer, Schiaparelli, and had the poise to wear this unusual evening dress with its painted lobster motif

👑 This Savile Row suit looks simple – but each detail was carefully planned by the Duke

♛ A fine calf handbag with a lizard-skin trimming. Many of Wallis's bags were decorated with a tiny crown and her monogram

Head-hugging hat, with flattering blue veil

Fitted jacket with two lines of buttons

Turn-back cuffs, lined to pick out check pattern

♛ How to travel in perfect style – the Duchess wore this suit and matching topcoat for a sea trip to the United States

♛ Superbly chic, this slim crêpe dress by Mainbocher is trimmed with contrasting bows. A simple pearl choker echoes the neckline

Bows for decoration only – the fastening at back

Very narrow skirt, slit to mid-calf with matching binding

♛ The Duchess had tiny feet, and her elegant shoes matched every outfit

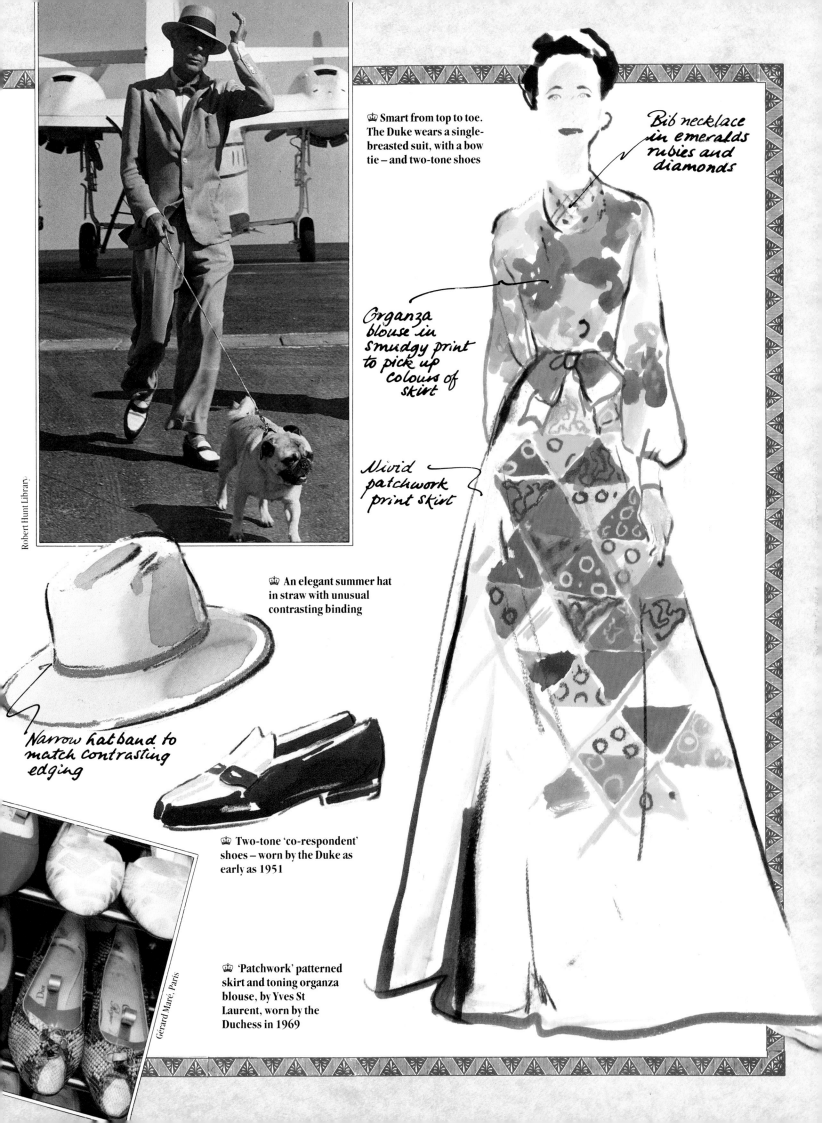

♛ Smart from top to toe. The Duke wears a single-breasted suit, with a bow tie – and two-tone shoes

Bib necklace in emeralds rubies and diamonds

Organza blouse in smudgy print to pick up colours of skirt

Vivid patchwork print skirt

♛ An elegant summer hat in straw with unusual contrasting binding

Narrow hat band to match contrasting edging

♛ Two-tone 'co-respondent' shoes – worn by the Duke as early as 1951

♛ 'Patchwork' patterned skirt and toning organza blouse, by Yves St Laurent, worn by the Duchess in 1969

Robert Hunt Library.

Gérard Maré, Paris

FOR THE WOMAN I LOVE

BY 1936, THE KING'S 'UNKNOWN COMPANION' HAD CAPTURED HIS HEART. BUT NOW THE SITUATION HAD CHANGED. DAVID HAD TO MAKE THE AGONIZING CHOICE BETWEEN MATRIMONY AND MONARCHY, DESIRE AND DUTY

T HE WEEK AFTER HIS FATHER'S DEATH, THE new King, Edward VIII, watched the celebrations welcoming him to the throne from the safety of St James's Palace. Beside him was Wallis, by now his constant companion. Speculation about the nature of her relationship with the new King was growing, although the British press had been instructed to give the affair a low profile. One famous caption referred to her simply as 'the King's unknown companion'.

From the very beginning, there had been indications that the new King's reign might pose problems. According to the age-old British tradition, postage stamps showed the successive monarchs in alternate profiles. Edward VIII's should have shown his right side. But he refused, feeling that his left profile was more photogenic. Unfortunately, the postal authorities forgot to change the background they had already prepared, with the result that the new King, instead of looking at the crown, faced away from it and into a shadow – a bad omen, many people thought.

Beset by problems

But this was only the beginning. The King had by now become totally obsessed with his predicament over Wallis. 'It was she who filled his thoughts at all times,' wrote a Palace official, 'she alone who mattered. Before her, the affairs of state sank into insignificance.' Edward often referred to his royal obligations as 'a relentless grind', and cared little for the dispatch boxes that contained official papers, frequently ignoring them or leaving them unattended. This neglect of duty – together with his increasing pro-German sympathies when war with Germany seemed likely – gave rise to great consternation. Fearing for national security, the Foreign Office took the unprecedented step of screening all the material that was sent to him.

♛ *Edward's duties as King included many visits to depressed areas – he is shown* left *visiting Glasgow. But, increasingly, his thoughts were of Wallis. Below* The first public picture of the couple.

Hulton-Deutsch Collection

Popperfoto

♛ **Above** *Postage stamps commemorating Edward VIII's accession to the throne. At the last minute, Edward refused to be photographed facing right, as requested. This, compounded by an error on the part of the postal authorities, meant that he was shown facing away from the crown instead of towards it, and into a shadow. In later years* The Times *was to single out the incident as being an 'apt symbol of a reign'*

The King's interest in Wallis took a heavy toll. Old friends were ignored and even his ever-faithful staff were shoddily treated. Much of the blame was heaped on Wallis, who, many people claimed, had an excessive influence over the King. Employees from the royal residences were suddenly sacked or forced to take salary cuts for 'economy reasons', and old retainers from the family estates were dismissed without thanks. It was hard for them to understand what was happening, because the King – the erstwhile Prince whom they had revered and loved – was all the while buying fabulous jewels for his American sweetheart. He was, quite literally, sparing no expense in his obsessive love.

Through these personally troubled times, the King's popular public profile in Britain remained untarnished and the people at large still worshipped him as the 'Great Communicator'. He was cheered on a memorable visit to the shipbuilders at Clydeside where he toured the *Queen Mary*, and his image with the common people remained undented.

Assassination attempt

During the Trooping of the Colour ceremony in 1936, however, an incident occurred which at first seemed to put his popularity in doubt – an attempt was made on his life. While reviewing the ranks of soldiers, a revolver was levelled at the King. A policeman deflected the assailant's arm, knocking the weapon out of his hand, before he had a chance to fire, but the news spread quickly. According to one South African correspondent's account: 'The King stared calmly into the would-be assassin's eyes before continuing with the ceremony.'

The man turned out to be a lunatic Scottish journalist called George McMahon. He was not seriously intent on trying to kill the King, but merely wanted to draw attention to a personal grievance. Ironically, the King's courage throughout the incident seemed only to increase his popularity with the people.

Although the King remained unruffled by the event on the parade ground and played golf later in the day, the world's press pronounced that he had had a 'God-given escape'. He received hundreds of messages congratulating him on his survival. One telegram came from Germany. Adolf Hitler's missive read: 'I have just received the news of the execrable attempt on Your Majesty. I beg to tender to Your Majesty my heartiest congratulations on your escape from this danger.'

On his deathbed, George V had prophesied that 'David will ruin himself within 12 months,' and his warning had a certain knowing tone. In fact, it was to take 11 months.

No-one knows exactly when the King – still David to his few friends – decided that he actually wanted to marry Wallis. Some people believe it was as early as 1934. In any event, in 1936 he asked Ernest Simpson to allow his wife, Wallis, to divorce him. Ernest's reactions were, not surprisingly, confused and angry, and it is rumoured that the two men actually came

Popperfoto

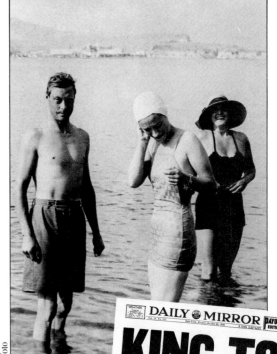

Popperfoto

ILN Picture Library

KING TO MARRY 'WALLY'
WEDDING NEXT JUNE

LONDON.—Within a few days Mrs. Ernest Simpson of Baltimore, Md., U. S. A., will obtain her divorce decree in England, and some eight months thereafter she will be married to Edward VIII, King of England.

King Edward's most intimate friends state with the utmost positiveness that he is very deeply and sincerely enamored of Mrs. Simpson, that his love is a righteous affection, and that almost immediately after the coronation he will take her as his consort.

(See later editions for detailed story and photographs)

(Continued on Page 18)

👑 *Edward and Wallis's Nahlin cruise in 1936 finally ended the speculation about their relationship and in the autumn the press erupted with news of the imminent marriage. A revealing letter from Wallis below indicates concern at her own public image in the event of his abdication*

Courtesy of Suzanne Blum-Spillman and Michael Bloch

to blows at one point during the heated quarrel.

But the odds were against Ernest – his wife was now deeply involved with the King and 'How do you argue with a King and his persuasion?' he later revealed. Eventually, on receiving an assurance from the King that he would marry Wallis, Ernest promised not to contest the divorce. Although he was by now seeing another woman, many people saw his agreement to the divorce under these conditions as a commendable desire to protect his wife's reputation.

In the summer of 1936, the King was determined to go away on holiday with Wallis, far from the British public eye. He arranged a cruise along the Dalmatian coast on a sleek new chartered yacht called *Nahlin*. Although the expedition was meant to be a private one, it soon became very public. The British press had promised not to cover the story, but the American and Continental press had no such restrictions. The cruise covered the Greek islands, Turkey and Yugoslavia, ending up at Vienna. Crowds gathered at their every port of call and the American and European press went wild with excitement. 'King to marry Wally' read the headlines. The couple were photographed in swimwear together which made sensational news. Wallis was even photographed in

> *'I do love you so entirely and in every way madly, tenderly, adoringly'*
>
> EDWARD, TO WALLIS

her négligé with a pyjama'd King beside her.

Wallis was overwhelmed by her sudden international fame, even though it was still not clear to her what the King's intentions were. The King, at the time, seemed blissfully unaware of the turmoil and gossip his relationship was generating. He loved his home country and enjoyed certain aspects of royalty – all he wanted to complete his life was to share the throne with his perfect woman, Wallis.

On their return from the *Nahlin* cruise, the King became aware that problems were brewing and said, 'I have no regrets for having chartered the *Nahlin*, though I may have been a bit indiscreet. Clouds seem to be rolling up – not only clouds of war but clouds of private trouble …' Wallis, for her part, became increasingly aware of their predicament and, without thought to her own feelings, pleaded with the King to forsake her.

Try as she might to return to her husband so that any potential disaster could be avoided, she was swayed by David who wrote: ' I do love you so entirely and in every way … Madly, tenderly, adoringly, and with admiration and such confidence.'

Wallis's harassed and burdened mind could hold out no longer and she capitulated to the King's desire.

CONSTITUTION IN CRISIS

Wallis had started divorce proceedings against her husband Ernest just before the summer cruise and, after their return, Stanley Baldwin, the Conservative Prime Minister, could no longer avoid the political crisis that was becoming imminent. He knew that the King was in love with an American divorcee, and he also recognized that she would be unacceptable as a queen. The King was 'Defender of the Faith', the Church saw every marriage as indissoluble and did not recognize divorce.

This was the theory and it was especially applicable to the King, who was, after all, supposed to be the spiritual leader of the nation. Baldwin also had to consider the feelings of the nations of the British Empire, an institution that had been nurtured on the foundation stone of a supreme monarchy that was beyond reproach. Because there was no written constitution in Great Britain, there was no way Baldwin could order the King not to marry – all he could do was point out the problems.

Enter the Prime Minister

Baldwin visited the King at Fort Belvedere and asked him to influence Wallis's divorce proceedings, to prevent them from going ahead. In this way, he hoped to make it legally impossible for the King to marry Wallis. Time was pressing – the date for the Coronation of Edward VIII had been set for 12 May 1937.

The King, infuriated by Baldwin's suggestion, retorted point-blank that, come what may, he intended to marry Wallis. But he was still hopeful that something could be done to ease

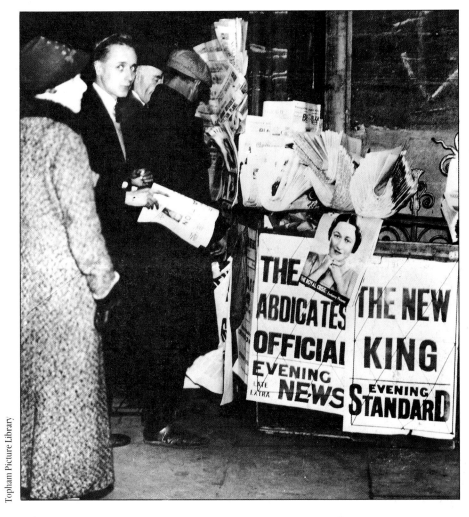

Topham Picture Library

👑 *With the signing of the Instrument of Abdication on Thursday 10 December 1936, King Edward VIII's short reign came to an end. At last, the months of agonizing were over.* Above *An anxious public flocks to the news stands*

his predicament. He contacted Lord Beaverbrook, the press magnate, who agreed to apply his massive influence over Fleet Street and guaranteed that nothing untoward would be published. The staunchly loyal Churchill also sided with the King and begged for time, in the hope that the crisis could be sorted out.

The road to abdication

Wallis's divorce, on the grounds of Ernest's adultery, was heard on 27 October 1936. It was reported – albeit matter-of-factly – in the local press, and this was sufficient to make it plain that a genuine crisis was imminent. The implications of the announcement were especially obvious to Major Hardinge, the King's Private Secretary, who formally wrote to the King, explaining that the press would not remain passive any longer. He also wrote that the Government was more than a little anxious to resolve the problem before it was forced to resign in face of the impossible situation.

On hearing Hardinge's message, the King sacked his hapless servant and hired a new Private Secretary, Walter Monckton, to act as go-between. The King confided in Monckton, an old Oxford friend, saying, 'As you know, my make-up is very different from that of my

THE POLITICAL SOLUTION

Edward was determined to marry Wallis before the Coronation, and so a morganatic marriage was seen as an answer to the crisis. But the Prime Minister, Stanley Baldwin *right*, saw that any solution which involved Wallis becoming the wife of the reigning monarch would cause uproar and put his government at risk. He disposed of the idea by putting it to the Dominions in such a way that they could only answer no. Ironically, with hindsight, there is nothing constitutionally improper about the monarch marrying a divorcee

Hulton-Deutsch Collection

father. I believe they would prefer someone more like him. Well, there is my brother Bertie.'

In November, the King saw Baldwin again and, for the first time, uttered the words that were to change history. '…I mean to abdicate to marry Mrs Simpson.' After the meeting, the King drove to visit his mother, Queen Mary, whose shocked reaction to the news served only to underline exactly how out of touch she really was with her son's affairs.

As a last resort, it was suggested to the King that a morganatic marriage might be possible. According to this 'agreement', Wallis, though married to the King, would not become Queen, and any children she might bear would not inherit the rights of succession to the throne. If this type of marriage had any appeal to David and Wallis, however, their optimism about it was short-lived. Baldwin and his cabinet put the proposition to the countries of the British Empire, wording it in such a way that only one answer could be forthcoming. As expected, Australia, Canada, New Zealand and South Africa were all in agreement. They did not want Mrs Simpson as Queen Consort, and agreed that the only solution for the King was to give up the idea of marrying or abdicate.

Wallis flees

Aunt Bessie, Wallis's ever-loving relative, was with her when the press finally broke the news – Lord Beaverbrook could hold back the hounds no longer. Wallis immediately decided to leave for France where she would stay with her friends Herman and Katherine Rogers, who had befriended her in Peking many years earlier. The journey through France was to be a nightmare for Wallis – the feverish press from every continent soon found her destination.

On the Friday after Wallis's departure, Winston Churchill, an old friend of the King, came to dinner at the Fort to lend his advice and counsel. A memorable evening passed with Churchill urging the King, with his soon-to-be-famous rhetoric, not to give in and surrender: 'We may win. We may not. Retire to Windsor Castle! Summon the Beefeaters! Raise the drawbridge! Close the gates! And dare Baldwin to drag you out!'

While staying with the Rogers in France, Wallis tried one last time to rectify the problem that had grown so rapidly out of control, and drafted a statement saying that she would leave the King: 'Mrs Simpson, throughout the last few weeks, has invariably wished to avoid any action or proposal which would hurt or damage His Majesty or the Throne.

'Today her attitude is unchanged, and she is willing, if such action would solve the problem, to withdraw from a situation that has been rendered both unhappy and untenable.'

Her statement came too late. The King was set on his course and the Instrument of Abdication had already been prepared.

Up to the last minute before the abdication, there was still much public support and sympathy for the King. Many of his close advisers felt that he could have remained King if he had understood the workings of the British constitutional system better. They felt that if he had taken more time before committing himself to marriage, a suitable compromise could have been worked out.

But the die had been cast, and for the King there was no turning back. Before he officially abdicated, he had to give the reins of power to his brother Bertie. It was decided that he should take the title of the Duke of Windsor and would receive a substantial annual income from the Crown. He agreed to help his brother as much as he could to make his accession easier. A period of two years absence from Britain was also agreed upon, before he could return – a promise which was to be broken.

The point of no return

On 10 December 1936, the King, after reigning for just 325 days, signed the Instrument of Abdication with three of his brothers as witnesses. As a consequence, the ill-prepared, shy Prince Albert, Duke of York, became King George VI.

The following day, David dined with his family before broadcasting his last message to the nation, in which he declared his intention to give up the throne for the woman he loved.

👑 *By 11 December 1936, Edward had abdicated and the crisis was over. In the evening, the former King above announced his decision to the nation. Wallis right meanwhile, unable to stand the strain, left for France*

FRIDAY, DECEMBER 11, 1936.

MRS. SIMPSON TOLD BY 'PHONE

London Call to Villa at Cannes

AFTER the news of the King's abdication had reached Cannes, Lord Brownlow stated that neither he nor Mrs. Simpson could make any statement on the matter.

It was thought possible, however (says Reuter), that a statement would be issued later.

News of the King's abdication reached the Villa Lou Viei from journalists at the same time as the news direct to Mrs. Simpson. She was then in her room on the top floor of the villa (says the B.U.P.), Mr. Herman Rogers at first reiterated emphatically that Mrs. Simpson was remaining in Cannes over Christmas, adding that the King was not expected to come to Cannes or anywhere else on the Riviera.

Later he told the British United Press that he was unwilling to say more than "Mrs. Simpson will remain here to-morrow."

When Mr. Rogers was asked: " Will the King marry Mrs Simpson?" he replied: "I cannot answer that."

"Can you say ' Yes' or ' No ?'" Asked. Mr. Rogers declared: "I cannot commit myself, but everything would indicate that this is the idea."

Fort Flag

John Frost

Hulton-Deutsch Collection

ILN Picture Library

THE ABDICATION SPEECH

"At long last I am able to say a few words of my own. I have never wanted to withhold anything, but until now it has been not constitutionally possible for me to speak.

A few hours ago I discharged my last duty as King and Emperor, and now that I have been succeeded by my brother, the Duke of York, my first words must be to declare my allegiance to him. This I do with all my heart.

You all know the reasons which have impelled me to renounce the throne. But I want you to understand that in making up my mind I did not forget the country or the Empire which as Prince of Wales, and lately as King, I have for twenty-five years tried to serve. But you must believe me when I tell you that I have found it impossible to carry the heavy burden of responsibility and to discharge my duties as King as I would wish to do without the help and support of the woman I love.

And I want you to know that the decision I have made has been mine and mine alone. This was a thing I had to judge entirely for myself. The other person most concerned has tried up to the last to persuade me to take a different course. I have made this, the most serious decision of my life, upon a single thought of what would in the end be the best for all.

This decision has been made less difficult for me by the sure knowledge that my brother, with his long training in the public affairs of this country and with his fine qualities, will be able to take my place forthwith, without interruption or injury to the life and progress of the Empire. And he has one matchless blessing, enjoyed by so many of you and not bestowed on me – a happy home with his wife and children.

During these hard days I have been comforted by my Mother and by my Family. The Ministers of the Crown, and in particular Mr Baldwin, the Prime Minister, have always treated me with full consideration. There has never been any constitutional difference between me and them and between me and Parliament. Bred in the constitutional tradition of my Father, I should never have allowed any such issue to arise.

Ever since I was Prince of Wales, and later on when I occupied the Throne, I have been treated with the greatest kindness by all classes, wherever I have lived or journeyed throughout the Empire. For that I am very grateful.

I now quit altogether public affairs, I lay down my burden. It may be some time before I return to my native land, but I shall always follow the fortunes of the British race and the Empire with profound interest, and if at any time in the future I can be found of service to His Majesty in a private station I shall not fail. And now we all have a new King, I wish him, and you, his people, happiness and prosperity with all my heart. God bless you all. God Save the King."

THE VILLA ON THE BOIS

*Secluded in Paris's Bois de Boulogne is a
magnificent château hidden behind high
rhododendron hedges. David and Wallis moved
there in 1953, just before the Duke's niece was
crowned Queen in Westminster Abbey, and it was to
remain their residence until the death of Wallis 33
years later. Granted to the couple by the City of Paris
for a token rent of 50 dollars a year, it was ideally
suited to the Duchess's love of entertaining. The
building is now being lovingly restored, with
everything just as the couple left it*

♛ *Above* The blue dining room showing its lavish silk
curtains and the set of three Meissen pots in the 'Flying
Tiger' pattern on the table. The wall panels *inset,
above right* were installed by the Duchess herself. The
Windsors hosted glittering dinner parties, employing
two chefs as well as a pastry cook, and among the wide
variety of guests were Lord Louis Mountbatten, Sir
Oswald Mosley and Cole Porter

♛ The imposing entrance hall *left and below*, with its
painted marble walls and classical ceiling. Hanging
from the balcony is a faded silk brocade banner
bearing the arms of the Prince of Wales, at one time
the possession of the Duke's grandfather. Below it, on
a gilt-legged table, is a red leather dispatch box marked
simply 'THE KING' – a poignant reminder of things
foregone

♔ A corner of the silver blue salon *right*. The embroidered Louis XVI chairs were part of the Duchess's extensive collection, much of which she bequeathed to the Palace of Versailles

♔ The Windsors' Paris residence was on the grounds of a private two-acre miniature park. As they were the only people allowed to live in the Bois, they had the entire park for their garden

Photographs by Gérard Maré, Paris

Derry Moore Photography

♛ Outside the library entrance *below*, the beloved pugs sit at the couple's feet and a collection of them, specially made in Meissen, sit on the table behind. In the library itself *bottom* a 1939 portrait of the Duchess hangs between the bookshelves. The yellow brocade sofa under the window was designed by Wallis herself

Horst/Hamilton Gallery

Gérard Maré, Paris

♛ The Duke's bathroom *left* is masculine and modern, with little ornament except regimental prints to embellish its veined marble walls. The bath itself was boarded over, since the Duke always preferred to take a shower

♛ The Duke's simple bedroom *right* is dominated by the hanging drape and bedspread which bear the motto of the Order of the Garter to which Edward belonged: *Honi soit qui mal y pense* – Evil to him who thinks evil

♛ The Duchess's bathroom *bottom right*. The ceiling's marquee-style stripes and tassels and the floral decorations on the walls make it a charming and summery room. A favourite Cecil Beaton drawing of the Duchess is reflected above the bath

♛ Even with its light-hearted set of pug cushions, the Duchess's bedroom is still a strikingly graceful and feminine room. It is full of daylight and decorated with watered silk wallpaper and gilded wheatsheaf mouldings

Derry Moore Photography

Gérard Maré, Paris

Gérard Maré, Paris

Cecil Beaton/Sotheby's

Popperfoto

Popperfoto

Popperfoto

Associated Press

MARRIAGE IN EXILE

HAVING RENOUNCED THE THRONE FOR THE WOMAN HE LOVED, THE DUKE WAS STILL UNABLE TO SEE WALLIS. BUT AFTER THE JOYFUL REUNION AND A MODEST WEDDING, THE EXILES STARTED THEIR SEARCH FOR A ROLE

Cecil Beaton/Camera Press

♔ *Left On his wedding day, the Duke looked out into an uncertain future with the woman for whom he renounced Crown and Empire, the strain of the past months etched permanently on his face.*

The marriage was a simple affair. Wallis was escorted by Herman Rogers (behind the bridal couple top left) and only a few friends were present. The Duke had supposed that his brothers would have been present as 'supporters', but the Palace was unbending in its disapproval and the trusty 'Fruity' Metcalfe (behind the Duke centre left) stood by faithfully.

The Rev Jardine inset left, who volunteered to marry the Duke and Wallis, was rewarded with a Bible inscribed 'Duke of Windor' below left. Later, he tried to assume the title 'The Duke's Vicar' and run a 'Windsor Cathedral' in Los Angeles

THE DAY AFTER DELIVERING HIS abdication speech, David crossed the English Channel to Boulogne on HMS *Fury*. As he sailed, it was announced by King George VI at his Accession Council that his elder brother would carry the title Duke of Windsor. As he started his self-imposed exile, it was not just his family and politicians who were relieved to see him go; most of his friends lost their interest in him overnight.

Much to their mutual frustration, the Duke and Wallis could not meet immediately. Lawyers had advised them that they should live apart until April 1937, when Wallis could expect to receive the final decree absolute of her divorce. So, when he arrived in France, the Duke and his retinue were driven to Austria to stay at Schloss Enzesfeld, a castle owned by Baron and Baroness Eugène de Rothschild.

Wallis, in the meantime, continued to stay with the Rogers at their villa near Cannes. Already, she had started to receive hate mail, the bulk of which came from women who appeared to be jealous of her catch. The press, too, were unkind.

She did, however, get one letter of consolation. 'My thoughts have been with you throughout your ordeal, and you may rest assured that no one has felt more deeply for you than I have.' It was from Ernest Simpson.

It was not long before the Duke assumed control of the castle and thought of his hostess as a guest in his home. He never thanked her for

> **'My duty was to evoke the nearest equivalent of a kingly life without a kingdom'**
>
> THE DUCHESS OF WINDSOR

her kindness and he was arrogant and bossy to the household staff she had provided for him. The Baron, who had remained in Paris, was also irritated. All the Duke's bills were being forwarded to him.

Although the Duke was not the multi-millionaire he claimed he should have been, he was certainly a rich man. He had also been given a handsome allowance by the King, but this did not quell his bitterness at being deprived of his interest in the family estates. Wallis shared these feelings and, during the endless telephone calls he made promptly at seven o'clock each evening, she tried to console him.

In March, both the Duke and Wallis moved to new temporary addresses. The Duke and his entourage took over a pension next to a lake near St Wolfgang and Wallis moved to the Château de Candé near Tours, where the couple would be married. The château was owned by Charles Bedaux who had made his fortune in America and who proudly proclaimed himself an 'out-and-out Fascist'. He had his eye on the potential of Nazi Germany and his plan was to ingratiate himself with the Duke, who had always admired Germany, as a means of coming to the notice of the Nazi leadership.

While they were separated, the Duke and Wallis kept in touch by telephone and copious letters to each other. At last they were reunited in May after Wallis's divorce became absolute. To Wallis's great sadness, Slipper, her favourite dog, was bitten by a poisonous snake the day

STARTING A LIFE-LONG HONEYMOON

As the Windsors drove off on their honeymoon in their Buick – the thrice-married bride strewing roses – they were cheered by crowds at every corner. 266 pieces of luggage, including 186 trunks, followed behind with a retinue of six.

In Venice, their first stop, the lovers played at being tourists – a ride down the Grand Canal by speedboat and in a gondola, and a stroll through St Mark's Square. And everywhere they went, they were mobbed by enthusiasts

Robert Hunt Library

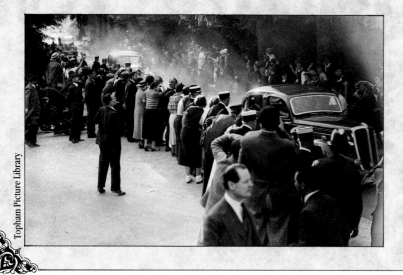

Topham Picture Library

♛ *The American press reacted to the wedding in true democratic style* below. *The tragedy was that though Wallis was well born by American standards, she could not comprehend the constitutional havoc she would have caused as Queen. And the Duke, aspiring to a more modern monarchy – he sported a transatlantic accent all his life – miscalculated his influence by confusing his personal identity with his symbolic role as Sovereign*

John Frost

before the Duke was to join her at Château de Candé, and died shortly afterwards. She saw it as an omen of bad news.

In spite of the Duke's requests, no member of his family would attend the wedding and the marriage would gain no official recognition – the Church of England wanted nothing to do with it. But a vicar from Darlington, the Rev Robert Anderson Jardine, was prepared to bless the couple in spite of his Bishop's express orders not to do so.

A Royal snub

But the most crushing blow of all was yet to come. The day before the wedding, the King sent a message. Wallis would not share her husband's royal status – she could call herself the Duchess of Windsor, but she was not to be addressed as Her Royal Highness.

The Duke was furious and tearful at the same time, and he was to remain embittered about this ultimate insult till he died. The reasoning seemed to be that since Wallis had been divorced twice before, she may divorce yet again, and it would be improper for her children to inherit a royal title.

In 1938, the Duke was advised by a top constitutional lawyer, Sir William Jowitt, that the King had acted illegally in withholding the title from the Duchess. The Duke was prevailed upon not to force the issue, however, as it would have precipitated a crisis throughout the Empire and, worse still for him, resurrected unpleasant details about Wallis's past. But long before this vindication, the Duke had ordered his

staff to address his wife as Her Royal Highness.

When the great day arrived, there was only a handful of friends at the château. The Rogers, the Moncktons, the Metcalfes, Baron and Baroness de Rothschild, and Aunt Bessie were among the few that were present. The atmosphere was hardly one befitting the 'Wedding of the Century', as it had been dubbed, but there were touches of splendour. Constance Spry provided the bouquets and floral decorations of lilies and white peonies and Cecil Beaton was asked to take the photographs, with the strict instruction that he was only to shoot the Duke's left profile. The celebrated organist, Marcel Dupré, provided the music.

Thoughtfully Wallis had by now changed her name back to Warfield by deed poll. She wore a long blue crêpe dress of 'Wallis blue' and a hat of tiny pink and blue feathers. On her wrist was a magnificent diamond and sapphire bracelet and, at her throat, a matching clasp – just two of the Duke's lavish gifts. The wedding ring itself was made of pure Welsh gold.

Married at last

As noon approached, the Mayor of Monts arrived to carry out the civil ceremony which was to precede the religious blessing. There was a moment of panic because the nervous Mayor had not asked for all the documents but, after just 12 minutes, he pronounced the couple 'united in the bonds of matrimony'.

After the civil ceremony, the Mayor retired and Dr Jardine, the renegade vicar, took over.

'Fruity' Metcalfe acted as best man and Wallis was escorted by Herman Rogers. The couple exchanged vows and, a few minutes later, the champagne corks popped. A buffet luncheon of chicken à la king – no joke was intended – was followed by wild strawberries and cream. As the evening drew closer, the Duke introduced the Wallis cocktail, a lethal concoction of Cointreau, peppermint, gin, lemon juice and soda.

Shortly after six o'clock that evening, the newlyweds were driven to the Italian border where they boarded a luxury railway coach that had been lent by Benito Mussolini. Among other things, the coach featured a bathroom and luxurious double bedroom. That night, as they travelled through northern Italy, the Duke donned red pyjamas and the Duchess a négligé of blue and silver lamé with a daringly low-cut back.

After Venice, tours of Milan and the Italian Riviera followed before the couple rested at the beautiful Austrian castle at Wasserleonburg which had been loaned to them by Count Paul Munster. From this idyllic setting, the Duke and Duchess roamed the countryside and visited local beauty spots.

At one point, it was supposed that the Duke and Duchess of Kent were going to visit them at the castle but when his sister-in-law, Princess Marina, refused to meet the newlyweds, the Duke was furious and gave his brother a dressing-down. This was the latest in a string of snubs that had been delivered by the Royal Family. The finger was pointed at his mother and at the Queen, who bitterly resented the Duke for forcing her husband, the stammering, shy and ill-equipped King, into a position that he found demanding and painful.

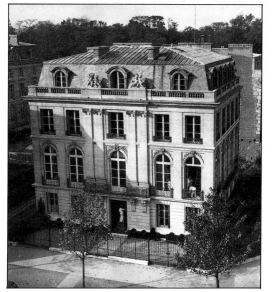

Robert Hunt Library

Hulton-Deutsch Collection

☙ *By 1938, with hopes of settling in England receding, the Windsors moved into 24 Boulevard Suchet, Paris. The Duchess immediately brought in the decorators. 'The question was whether we should conduct ourselves like fugitives, always on the run, or put on a show of our own,' she said. 'David was born to be a king; he had been a king. In marriage the palaces were lost . . . and my duty, as I saw it, was to evoke for him the nearest equivalent to a kingly life that I could produce without a kingdom'*

THE WINDSORS IN GERMANY

The Windsors visited Nazi Germany in 1938 *below*, unwitting stooges of Charles Bedaux, a scheming American. In factories, they were hailed, 'Heil Windsor', to which they returned, 'Heil Hitler'. However, the Führer thought it his prerogative to be late for their meeting *right*: an abdicated King could be left waiting. Wallis, who knew no German, appeared the perfect consort

Hulton-Deutsch Collection

IN SEARCH OF A ROLE

After excursions to Hungary and Czechoslovakia, the Duke and Duchess travelled to Paris where they rented a two-bedroom suite at the Hotel Meurice. Their three-month honeymoon was over and they now looked about them for something to do. The Duke, in particular, assumed that it was only a matter of time before they would both be accepted back in England. He dreamed of living once again at his beloved Fort where they would be surrounded by familiar countryside and friends. He also sought an official post of some kind which would keep him occupied. He had his eye on the Governor-Generalship of Canada, but was oblivious to the fact that, although he was fond of the Canadians, they were bitterly disappointed in him and the nation had been truly upset by his abdication.

A meeting with Hitler

It was Charles Bedaux – the millionaire who had offered his château for the marriage – who then proposed a trip to Germany.

Bedaux was a self-proclaimed Fascist who, faced with the reversal of his fortunes in the United States, saw his future in Nazi Germany, where his approach to mechanized production was well received. He saw his 'friends', the Duke and Duchess of Windsor, as his golden opportunity to ingratiate himself.

Not surprisingly, the Duke and Duchess were well received wherever they went in Germany during the autumn of 1937. The climax of their tour was an audience with the Führer at Berchtesgaden, his private hide-out in the foothills of the Alps. The couple had already met Himmler and Goering, and other names that were soon to ricochet around the world as 'mere terms of death'.

Reports of the German tour made headline news in all the major newspapers in Great Britain and America. Germany was rearming its war machine and the threat of war was becoming increasingly evident. Because of the press coverage, it was small wonder that the Duke issued a statement, cancelling their intended visit to America which was to have been sponsored by Bedaux.

The statement read: 'His Royal Highness arrived at his decision ... with great deliberation, but he feels that owing to the grave misconceptions which have arisen ... in regard to the motives and purposes of his industrial tour, there is no alternative but to defer it.' However, no matter what he said, it was believed his loyal-

Hulton-Deutsch Collection

♛ When World War 2 broke out, Mountbatten was sent to escort the Windsors back to Britain. The visit caused a stir among pressmen above, but no Royal welcome or hospitality awaited them. Instead, they were put up by the Metcalfes in Sussex

Popperfoto

Roger Viollet

♛ All dressed up and nowhere to go. Bereft of a role, the Windsors had little to do in France during the War. Wallis helped out in the Women's Ambulance Corps above right, and David made a few trips to the front above

ties were divided between King and country, self-made millionaires and Fascism.

The wandering Windsors

The Duke and Duchess roamed from hotel to house and back to hotel during their first years in Paris. For a time, they were reluctant to buy a home while there was still a possibility of returning to England. They took on long leases for two properties – one in Paris at 24 Boulevard Suchet, the other, a villa known as La Croë, at Cap d'Antibes.

When World War 2 broke out in September 1939, King George VI and Neville Chamberlain, the Prime Minister, soon learned that the Duke was agitating for work. In desperation, two propositions were put forward: the Duke could either become Assistant Regional

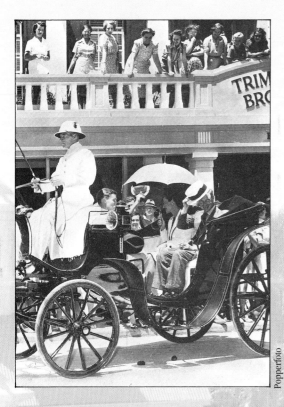

♛ *Posted to the Bahamas, the Duke and Duchess stopped on the way at Bermuda* left. *They arrived in the Bahamas in stifling heat that made the Duke uncomfortable as he took the Oath of Allegiance* below, *but Wallis maintained her regal composure*

Popperfoto

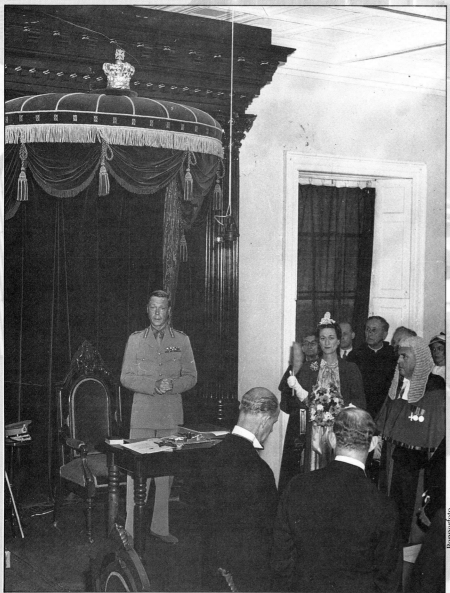

Popperfoto

Commissioner for Wales or Liaison Officer with the British Military Mission in France.

The Duke opted for the job of Regional Commissioner, but no sooner had he accepted the position than he was rejected. The Queen (the present Queen Mother) swayed influence on the decision – she, it was claimed, sought to protect her husband, the King, from the Windsors' ambitions. So, as soon as the Duke arrived in England, he was sent away again as a Major-General to the Military Mission.

The Duchess remained unruffled. She continued to shop for shoes, diamonds and dresses. But the Duke, to his infinite credit, crossed boundaries that had been 'forbidden' by the French Command. He visited the Maginot Line as the legendary *Prince de Galles* (Prince of Wales) and, thereafter, his welcome by the French troops was assured.

When France fell to the German forces, the Duke and Duchess fled, first to Spain and from there to Portugal, both neutral countries. The new premier of England, Winston Churchill, cabled his erstwhile friend in Lisbon, begging him and his wife to come back to England. But while the country suffered its gravest hours, the Duke adamantly refused to return unless two conditions were met: first, his wife was to be recognized as Her Royal Highness and, secondly, the King and Queen should receive them – requests that were not then to be granted.

A refuge in the sun

In the nick of time, a solution was found 'to keep the Windsors out of the way'. The Duke was appointed Governor of the Bahamas. It had been rumoured that Fascist organizers in Spain were trying to enlist the Duke's support and that the German Government had plans to reinstate him as King as soon as it gained supremacy.

Banished to the Bahamas, the Duke did his best and turned on the charismatic magic that had once made him such a popular figure. He endeavoured to make provisions for the old and young, and he looked into the chronic housing problems that afflicted the people. However, it was not long before the U-boat casualties arrived in droves and Wallis played an admirable role as President of the Red Cross. Shortly afterwards, she ran a canteen for American servicemen and soon won the admiration and love of the men-at-arms.

In March 1945, the Duke of Windsor resigned as Governor of the Bahamas, much to the surprise of everyone on the islands. His immediate aims were unclear. He had toyed with the idea of acting out his life story for the Hollywood movie cameras, but he realized that this would only alienate him further from his family – the last thing he wanted for Wallis.

Anne Bolt

WALLIS AND EDWARD, WITH LOVE

An extraordinary sacrifice had been made, a fundamental clash between duty and passion, and the result was a marriage that lasted 35 years. With the ordeal of the Abdication behind them, Wallis and David began a new and infinitely more private life in Paris. Without children, the couple's attention was lavished upon the cluster of dogs that lived with them and also upon the things of elegance and beauty with which they filled their mansion. Many of these objects had intimate inscriptions

♔ The Royal seal *left* in chalcedony and gold was one of a set of ten historical seals that the Duke had collected. It is engraved with the Prince of Wales feathers, until 1936 his personal cipher

"PREEZIE"

A FAITHFUL LITTLE FRIEND

OF

EDWARD AND WALLIS

DUKE AND DUCHESS OF WINDSOR

1938 - 1949

David from Harry

♔ The Duke and Duchess showed an enduring affection for dogs. Wallis *top left* holds Slipper, a cairn terrier whose death they marked with a Cartier medallion *inset*. A headstone *left* marks the passing of another favourite dog. A series of pug mementoes *above* held pride of place in the Duchess's bedroom

♔ The Duke's smoking kit *right* included gifts from his own close family. From his father, George V, is a silver cigarette case given to David in 1921 at the outset of his journey to India. The engraved match case is a 23rd birthday present from David's younger brother, Harry, Duke of Gloucester

ILN Picture Library

Robert Hunt Library

Gerard Maré, Paris

Sotheby's

♛ The Duke's bedroom was kept as a virtual temple by Wallis *right*; every inch of table space – even the tops of the chairs – carried photographs of her. Some were informal snapshots, but often David commissioned illustrious society photographers such as Man Ray and Cecil Beaton to have her pose for them. And yet all the time there was the nagging knowledge, as Lord Tennyson's framed quotation must always have reminded him, that no one would normally be asked to pay the price of such single-minded devotion

Derry Moore Photography

Sotheby's

♛ A gold cigarette case *above* from Wallis to David, 1935, and in return a gem-set powder compact. On the reverse of each are maps of shared romantic holidays

♛ Bought during her stay in the Far East in 1924, the Chinese doll *right* was one of the few souvenirs Wallis kept before meeting David

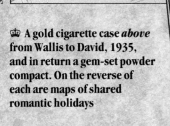

Derry Moore Photography

♛ The Duke kept the plaque *below* as a memento of his three months in the Royal Navy when he was 17

Sotheby's

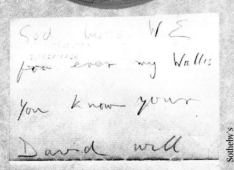

God bless WE
from ever my Wallis
you know your
David will
love you and
look after you so
long as he has breath
in this warm body

Courtesy of Suzanne Blum-Spillman and Michael Bloch

H.R.H. PRINCE EDWARD OF WALES. R.N.

Sotheby's

♛ This extract from a 1935 letter to Wallis shows just how passionate and intense the Windsor romance was. By bonding their first initials together they formed the single word – WE

♛ The halcyon days before George V's death brought on the storm of abdication were inevitably treasured by the Duke and Duchess. The photograph of them bathing in the sea *right* was a particular favourite

Sotheby's

♛ The Duchess's two-layered pearl necklace *below*. The inner string, made from natural pearls and joined by an oval diamond clasp, was a gift of reconciliation from Queen Mary, while the outer string, made from cultured pearls, was bought in Paris in 1964. The black and white earrings were worn by Wallis to her husband's funeral in 1972

♛ Each of the nine crosses in the jewelled bracelet *above* carries an inscribed message marking a moment of special significance in the couple's relationship, or simply a mutual declaration of love

♛ The bracelet *below* which Wallis wore at her wedding in June 1937 is made with baguette diamonds and cushion-set sapphires. Its clasp carries the inscription: 'For our contract 18-v-37'

♛ Four bracelets and a necklace had to be broken up to make this flamingo brooch *left* which David gave to Wallis in 1940. The plumage is studded with diamonds, rubies and emeralds, the eyes are of sapphire and the beak made of sapphire and citrine

👑 The dazzling diamond and ruby necklace *right* was a 40th birthday present from David. Its inscription 'My Wallis from her David' was typical of his fervent gestures of loyalty to her at the time of the Abdication Crisis

👑 The stained blue chalcedony set of jewels *above* shows the Duchess's love of the unconventional in decorative design

👑 The extravagant and sensual panther jewels *above* were made by Cartier. The stretched-out beast is a bracelet bought in 1952, with eyes of emerald and a pelt of diamonds and onyx

👑 An amethyst and turquoise lattice necklace, studded with diamonds and designed by Cartier in 1947. The Windsors' patronage of the famous jewellery house created an exquisite and unique collection of 'rival Crown Jewels', the scale of which only fully came to light at their auction in Geneva in 1987

YEARS OF EMPTINESS

THE WAR OVER, THE WINDSORS HAD TO SETTLE FOR AN ENDLESS ROUND OF PARTIES AND TRAVEL. FINALLY, IN THEIR TWILIGHT YEARS, THEY RECEIVED ROYAL RECOGNITION

On their return from the Bahamas in 1945 the Windsors discovered their Paris home had been sold by the owners. After staying at the Ritz for some time, the Duchess rented 85 Rue de la Faisanderie, conveniently situated in the centre of Paris below

WHEN THE WAR ENDED IN THE SUMMER of 1945, the Windsors visited New York as they could not yet get a passage back to France. The social life there suddenly blossomed into jubilant celebrations. The couple eagerly joined in the festivities and they regularly frequented night-clubs and high-society parties. While in New York, they stayed at the Waldorf-Astoria which was ideally sited for Wallis's shopping sprees in the fashionable parts of town. As each day went by, Wallis's wardrobe grew – something that was quickly picked up by the press, who wrote obsessively, and not always sympathetically, of her exploits. When the Duke and Duchess sailed for France after visiting President Truman, the noted columnist, Walter Winchell, who had taken to calling the Windsors 'the Dook and Dookess' wrote: 'Good riddance to them both – the snobs.'

When the Windsors arrived in Paris, they were shocked to find that their home on the Boulevard Suchet had been sold. However, the new owner had no objection to them staying there until they found a new address. Although everything was intact there – the German occupation had left everything untouched – the war and life in Nassau had evidently changed the Windsors. Lady Diana Cooper, the celebrated beauty, noted, 'The two poor little old things were almost pathetic. Fear, I suppose, of losing their youthful figures, or homesickness, has made them both Dachau-thin. She is much commoner and more confident, he much duller and sillier.'

Back to England

In October 1945, the Duke travelled to England to visit his mother whom he had not seen for nine years. To nobody's surprise, the Duchess was not invited, so she stayed in Paris and spent much of her time shopping. While in London, the Duke approached the new Foreign Secretary, Ernest Bevin, with the proposal that he might be made an 'ambassador-at-large' in the United States. He was determined to do something for his country, thinking that he could use his connections on both sides of the Atlantic to promote harmony and understanding between the British and American peoples. Ernest Bevin was concerned about the Duke's mistakes in the past – his fraternization with Hitler, his Fascist friends and the mixed term in the Bahamas. He therefore did not recommend the Duke to the Prime Minister, Clement Attlee, for a suitable position. The notion also found little sympathy with the Royal Family. In January 1946, the Prime Minister announced to the House of Commons that there was no 'job' for the Duke of Windsor. He was to try again in 1948 and 1951 for a suitable position, but again his requests met with a blanket refusal.

Reconciled to lives in exile, the Windsors listlessly wandered to and from their homes in Paris and the Cap d' Antibes in the south of France. Spending money and lavish partying became their way of life. In an account by the American writer, Susan Mary Alsop, the Duke was disconsolate: 'He is so pitiful, I never saw a man so bored. He said to me, "You know what my day was today? … I got up late and then I went with the Duchess and watched her buy a hat."'

But if their life style was increasingly aimless, the love between the couple grew stronger. Noël Coward, who had always been suspicious of their affair, noted in his diary after a party: 'Sat next to Wallis. She was charming and rather touching. He loves her so much, and at long last I am beginning to believe that she loves him.' In another entry, he added: 'They are lovers, so perhaps there is something to be said for the whole set-up. I wonder how their story will end.'

'A fool would know . . .'
During the autumn of 1946, the Windsors both travelled to England where they stayed with the Earl and Countess of Dudley. Nobody knew exactly how to treat the couple, because Wallis's status was still highly sensitive. Before inviting them over for cocktails one evening, the Duchess of Westminster is reported to have instructed her other guests: 'Remember now, you've all got to curtsey to him, but not to her.'

Scandal and publicity were never far behind the Windsors and, one evening, when the Duke and Wallis were dining out in London, there was a burglary at Ednam Lodge, the Dudleys' home. Nothing else was touched except Wallis's jewellery, nearly all of which was stolen, and the *Daily Mail* was one of the first newspapers to announce that it was valued at more than half a million pounds. The Duke denied this, and said that it was only valued at £20,000.

This statement provoked attacks from the American press who said that it had to be worth at least £250,000 because the Duke had settled a bill at Cartier's for £120,000 just after his abdication. Wallis added fuel to the fire when she replied to a reporter's question about the jewels she had been wearing on the night of the theft: 'A fool would know that with tweeds or other daytime clothes one wears gold, and that with evening clothes one wears platinum.' This hardly endeared her to the British public, who were suffering post-war rationing at the time.

Hulton-Deutsch Collection

Although insurance money enabled some of the jewels to be replaced, some were unique, including priceless uncut emeralds which had been left to the Duke by his grandmother on the understanding that they would one day be worn by a Queen of England. The Royal Family had always claimed that these emeralds were the property of the Crown and should have been left behind after the abdication.

Palm Beach royalty
Towards the end of 1946, the Duke and Duchess crossed the Atlantic once more. After visiting New York, they travelled south to Palm Beach in Florida, where the rich gathered to

♚ *In October 1945, Edward travelled to England to see his mother for the first time in nine years. Queen Mary above was to die eight years later in 1953. He also used the trip to approach the Government for a suitable foreign posting, but was flatly refused*

♚ *The Duke became resigned to never working for his country again. With so much free time, he and the Duchess started to travel in earnest. They are seen below by their custom-built station wagon in Palm Beach, Florida*

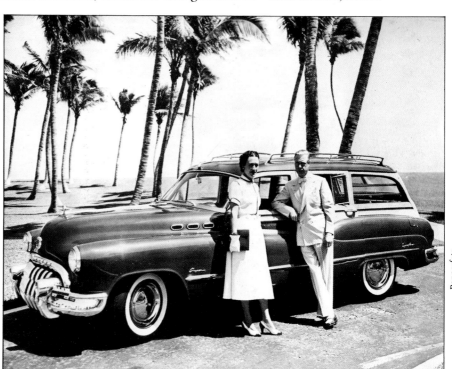

Popperfoto

spend the winter months away from the cold, northern climes. The Windsors were accepted in Palm Beach as true royalty; they were fêted by the brash millionaires and invitations to parties flowed in. At dinners, guests were instructed to bow or curtsey and nobody could leave until the Royal couple had first said their goodbyes. On one occasion, a flustered hostess was obliged to say to the Duke, who enjoyed chatting after a meal, 'Sir, some of the others are beginning to look awfully tired. Why don't you pretend to say good night, drive around the block for a bit, and then come back after the others have gone?'

While in the United States, the Duke sold the rights of his memoirs, which he had yet to write, to *Life* magazine for a sum reputed to be in six figures. This lead to rumours that the Windsors were hard up but, in truth, the Duke wanted a 'project' that would occupy his empty days. He set aside the summer of 1947 to write the book with his ghost writer, Charles Murphy, but because of his lack of concentration and constant interruptions from the Duchess, it was not published until 1951.

After six months, relaxing in the sunshine of Florida, the Duke and Duchess returned to Paris to receive another snub from the Royal Family – they were not invited to the wedding of Princess Elizabeth and Philip Mountbatten. Later in the year, while talking to reporters, Wallis said of the rebuff, 'It was purely a family matter,' adding a personal snipe at the Queen Mother: 'People should wear skirts at the length most becoming.'

The Windsors' discontent with life was ill-disguised. They found it impossible to settle down in any one country, as they continually travelled across the Atlantic. One year, they rented a vast house in Locust Valley, Long Island, the next they gave up the lease on their property on the Côte d' Azur because, as the Duchess said, 'The riffraff have taken over the

ILN Picture Library

Topham Picture Library

👑 *Even in exile the Duke and Duchess had a glamorous and extravagant life style. In the 1950s they were often flying abroad to parties with flamboyant friends such as Jimmy Donahue left, centre. They frequently travelled to the United States, and the Duchess's love of fashion is evident below as she is seen modelling a Parisian dress and cape at the Duchess of Windsor's Charity Ball at the Waldorf-Astoria in New York in 1953*

Popperfoto

Riviera.' Even their unfailing loyalty to each other became suspect because a new and devastating character entered their lives. His name was Jimmy Donahue and he was related to the 'five and dime store' Woolworth family.

Jimmy Donahue was an unrepentant homosexual who had captivated New York society; he was outrageously 'camp', immensely rich and undeniably witty and charismatic. The Duke and Duchess met him in Palm Beach at his mother's house in the spring of 1950 and were both captivated by his enigmatic personality. In the autumn of 1950, Wallis went to New York, while the Duke remained working on his book in Paris. News soon reached him through press cuttings that Jimmy Donahue was accompanying her wherever she went. On the face of it, the liaison appeared to be harmless enough: a 35-year-old homosexual could hardly threaten the marriage of a 54-year-old Duchess. But the Duke read the accounts back home in Paris and, alarmed by their implications, immediately set sail for New York. Wallis greeted him warmly on the gangplank of the *Queen Elizabeth* and, to reassure the press that all was well, they posed, kissing, for photographers. However, this did not mean the immediate departure of Jimmy Donahue from their lives. Far from it, the three of them went everywhere together. This was more than a little surprising because the Duke, unlike his wife, had always expressed a dislike for homosexuals.

Donahue even joined their retinue when they were in Paris and, when the Windsors moved out of their Boulevard Suchet home and into a rented house at 85 rue de la Faisanderie, it was Jimmy who helped Wallis organize the decorating schemes. He also escorted her to parties, staying late with her when the Duke was unwilling to do so.

Death of the King

This was undoubtedly a difficult time for the Duke, because, quite apart from worrying about his wife's activities, the Royal Family was going through troubled times. At the beginning of 1952, King George VI died. Although they were never particularly close as brothers, the Duke was deeply saddened as he felt he had always been loyal to 'Bertie'. At the funeral, he followed the pall bearers as a member of the Royal Family – the Duchess was not invited.

The following year, Princess Elizabeth was crowned Queen. The Duke had been invited to the Coronation but the Duchess had not, so neither went. Instead they watched the ceremony in Paris on television.

In the spring of 1953, the Duke was again summoned to England to attend the funeral of his mother, Queen Mary. As usual Wallis was not invited and on the night of the funeral is said to

Frank Scherse/Time Life Inc/Colorfic

have been seen dancing at a nightclub in New York with none other than Jimmy Donahue.

In 1953, the French Government offered the Windsors a grand mansion on the edge of the Bois de Boulogne in Paris. The prestigious villa had once been occupied by Charles de Gaulle and the massive, three-storey building was to become their main home for the rest of their lives.

A home at last

With her immaculate taste, the Duchess transformed the 'villa on the Bois' from a rundown town house to a sumptuous residence. But this was not the only house she had to restore because the Duke, with his overwhelming love of the countryside, had bought

The Duke and Duchess adored their French country home near Paris, the Moulin de la Tuilerie. As Wallis supervised the interior decorations, Edward lovingly tended the garden

In 1962, David and Wallis bought a plot of land at Los Monteros near Marbella in southern Spain with the intention of building a retirement home. Sadly, the subsequent ill health of the Duke made them abandon the project

Popperfoto

a beautiful farm house not far from Paris called the Moulin de la Tuilerie.

While Wallis attended to the interior decoration of the two houses, the Duke replanned the gardens, particularly the one in the country. His aim was to create an informal English garden in the heart of France – a project that was to take him two years, but which kept him relatively content.

In the mid-1950s, the Windsors' globetrotting life style began to slow down but it did not grind to a halt. They still loved entertaining as lavishly as in the old days and their friends frequently visited them.

In 1955, Wallis decided to follow in her husband's footsteps by writing a book. She hired Cleveland Amory as her 'editorial adviser', but he was soon fired because he did not agree with her approach – in his opinion, she only wanted to tell half a story. He said, 'I told the Duchess that I didn't mind omitting facts. But I wouldn't distort them. She wanted a soap opera.' Eventually, another ghostwriter was found and *The Heart Has Its Reasons* was published in the spring of 1956.

Old age and recognition

Towards the end of the 1950s, the Duke and Duchess grew more conscious of the passing of time. He was, by now, becoming increasingly deaf and she was obsessively worried about her figure. She hired a masseuse to pummel her waistline, but the problem was mostly imaginary. After attending a party at the Windsors' during this time, Noël Coward jotted in his diary: 'The conversation was mostly general and largely devoted to the question of whether or not the Duchess should have her face lifted. The main consensus was "no". Wallis brought this subject up herself with a sort of calculated defiance.'

Wallis did, in fact, have several facelifts to slow down the ageing process and, in 1965, the Duke visited London to have a series of operations to help save his failing sight. While he was recuperating in hospital, Queen Elizabeth visited her uncle and, at the same time, she met Wallis.

As if to consolidate the 'thawing' of the long family feud, the Queen invited the Duke and Duchess of Windsor a couple of years later to a ceremony to mark the centenary of Queen Mary's birth. For the very first time, the Duke and his wife, whom he adored so completely, were officially welcomed as a couple in England. At the unveiling of the memorial statue, the Queen Mother and the Duchess shook hands and exchanged a few words; but sharp eyes noted that the Duchess did not curtsey to the Queen Mother.

In 1970, Cecil Beaton was a guest at the Windsors' home in the Bois de Boulogne. He wrote in his diary: 'She [the Duchess] seems to

👑 *As he entered his seventies, the Duke's health began to decline and in March 1965 he entered the London Clinic for an eye operation. Both he and the Duchess, who accompanied him, were heartened by a visit from the Queen during his stay*

have suddenly aged, to have become a little old woman … the Duke, in a cedar-rose-coloured velvet golf suit, appeared. His walk with a stick makes him into an old man.'

By November 1971, the Duke had been diagnosed as having inoperable throat cancer, but neither he nor the Duchess had been told exactly what was the matter. In May 1972, the Queen, the Duke of Edinburgh and Prince Charles visited the Duke, after being informed that he was a dying man. Although he was very weak, had been bedridden for some time and could only talk in the faintest of whispers, he insisted that he would get up to greet his niece. So, dressed in a startling jacket that disguised the true state of his body, he got out of bed. His effort clearly drained his reserves, and he was helped back to bed, never to leave it again. Eight days later the Duke died.

👑 *On 7 June 1967, the Duke and Duchess were both invited to London by the Queen to the unveiling of a plaque at Marlborough House to commemorate the centenary of the birth of the Duke's mother, Queen Mary. This was the first time that the Duchess had been given official Royal approval. In the Royal gathering are from left to right: the Queen, the Queen Mother, the Duke and Duchess of Gloucester and the Duke and Duchess of Windsor*

Hutton-Deutsch Collection

EXILED NO MORE

When the Queen heard of the Duke of Windsor's death on 28 May 1972, she ordered nine days of official court mourning. His coffin *above*, bearing a single wreath from Wallis, was flown from Paris to England and was laid in state at St George's Chapel, Windsor, as the Duke wished. During the private funeral service, conducted by the Dean of Windsor, the heavily sedated Duchess *below* could hardly raise her head as she sat between the Queen and the Duke of Edinburgh. The Duke was laid to rest at Frogmore in the Royal burial ground

John Frost

Daily Mail

Duchess of Windsor will fly back with him in RAF plane-and accepts Queen's invitation to stay at Buckingham Palace

THE KING WHO CHOSE LOVE

Daily Mail special coverage and picture documentary—see Page 2 and Pages 13, 14 and 15

THE DUKE COMES HOME

THE DUCHESS OF WINDSOR will fly in the RAF plane bringing the body of the Duke back to England on Wednesday.

Popperfoto

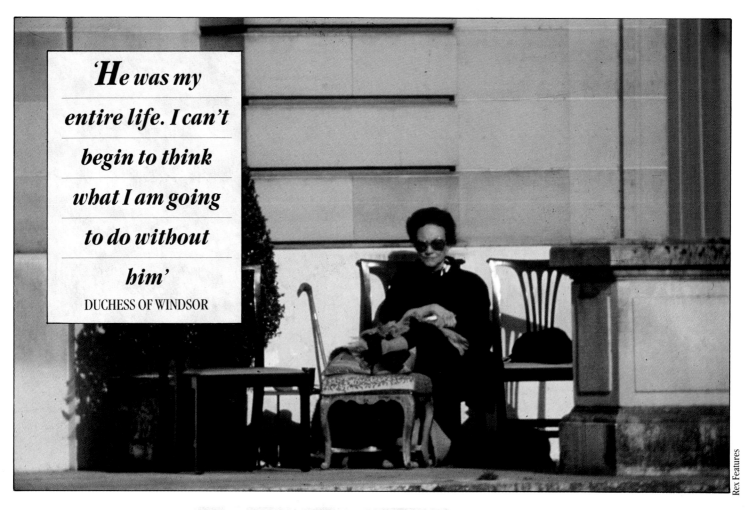

'*He was my entire life. I can't begin to think what I am going to do without him*'
DUCHESS OF WINDSOR

Rex Features

♔ *Wallis was devastated by David's death but, despite her deteriorating health, she lingered alone for another 14 years. She died on 24 April 1986 and was laid to rest beside her David at Frogmore, Windsor*

John Frost

THE DUCHESS MOURNS

For the first few weeks after the Duke's funeral, Wallis was kept sedated and she remained indoors with only her dogs for company. But she did have some consolations: Queen Elizabeth the Queen Mother, the one member of the family who had opposed her for so long, had written to her and had signed the note informally, 'Elizabeth', as opposed to the more formal 'Elizabeth R'. In a similar vein of reconciliation, the Queen Mother had gone out of her way to console Wallis during her brief stay at Buckingham Palace, prior to the Duke's funeral.

As the long and lonely years passed, the Duchess's mind became confused. She had been suffering from arteriosclerosis for some time and became increasingly suspicious of people and, at times, totally obsessed with money. When Lord Louis Mountbatten visited her and suggested that she might like to set up a Duke of Windsor Foundation to help needy causes in Britain, she

was initially very keen on the idea. In the end, the answer was 'no' and she hired a French lawyer, Maître Suzanne Blum, to look after all her legal and financial affairs.

In 1973, an ugly and unnecessary rumour was printed by the French newspapers that Wallis was about to marry for the fourth time. The man in question was one of her private secretaries, John Utter. To those who knew them both, the story was obviously untrue, because they actively disliked each other. Shortly afterwards, Utter resigned, unable to cope with Wallis's increasingly unpredictable temper which would flare up for no apparent reason.

Over the years Wallis's health deteriorated further, as she became beset with gastric and liver problems that prevented her from eating and drained her strength. By 1978 she was totally bedridden. Emaciated and ghostlike, she lay in a huge bed, tended day and night by nurses. She was unable to read or watch the television. But, although her life was empty and pitifully sad, she lived on for eight more years until her death on 24 April 1986. The Queen, Prince Philip and Queen Elizabeth the Queen Mother were among those that attended her short funeral service at St George's Chapel, Windsor. Her body was laid to rest beside that of her adoring husband, David, at Frogmore.